How Death
Came into
the World

How Death Came into the World
Nancy Charley

Smokestack Books
1 Lake Terrace, Grewelthorpe, Ripon HG4 3BU
e-mail: info@smokestack-books.co.uk
www.smokestack-books.co.uk

Copyright 2020,
Nancy Charley,
all rights reserved.

Cover image:
Arthur Rackham,
Bird on a Lantern

ISBN 9781916139244

Smokestack Books
is represented
by Inpress Ltd

Contents

Hallowed Ground	11
Foxed	13
How Death Came into the World	14
Approaching her Birthday	15
Eyrie	16
How Death Came into the World	17
Mantle	18
Not your Daughter	19
Talis-woman	20
Not your Daughter	21
Why Drink Lemonade when the Lemons are so Juicy	22
How Death Came into the World	23
The Gap Year Trek of Tracey Short	24
No Silver Lining	25
How Death Came into the World	26
Flight Feathers and Bone	27
Ballend Pool	28
Lifted	30
Classification: *Ursus consolativus*	31
How Death Came into the World	32
Running	33
July 23rd	34
Prey Bird as Neighbour	35
Rule	36
How Death Came into the World	37
Coppicing	38
Constrictive Pericarditis	39
To See Through a Glass Darkly	40
Monday's Child is Fair of Face	41
Reclassification	42
How Death Came into the World	43
Triptych	44
The Plunderer	48
Deathblow	50
The Elizabethan Coast	51

How Death Came into the World	52
A Stitch in Time	53
A Thanet Fable	54
Hooden Horsing Around	56
As Luck Would Have It	57
How Death Came into the World	59
Strand	60
The Weed-Reaper	61
In this Frostless Land	62
Jack	63
Winter's Code	65
Laid Bare	67
How Death Came into the World	69
Reflection	70
Acknowledgements	71

Hallowed Ground

When October rains fill the drains,
Will wisp stirrers rise again.

Heavenshard rain
                       turns path to slosh
sobbed and graimed
                      she skelters indoors.

Settled in her study
                      the lit lamp floods
     over fugitive stories

lost in loss's compelling words.

        Suddenly skeer'd
by skitter on roof.
           Magpie? Collared doves?

All Hallows Eve sets souls unleashed,
One for sorrow, two for peace.

Muted mizzle
                      is pulse's rhythm.

The window frames
                 a waning moon
      ochre burr forecasts
                      hasty rain soon.

Live loosing loss.
> Breath bristles her neck,

'She'll do.
> Albert Zion, I'll rest with you.'

An absence
> fills the room.

A woman cannot rest or roam
Till she trusts another with her home.

Foxed

All day the scruff-brush vixen whelp
lurks in the charnel of carnage.
This week has yielded
      twenty starlings, three harvest mice,
a well-seasoned crow, four fledged wrens,
two voles and a snarky water-rat
   whose lashing claws
caused the sore on the whelp's forepaw
for which she sporadically raises her head,
      licks its crust,
before resuming her guarded crouch.

Sometimes she dreams of her mother's teat,
imagines her yelp in the east wind's howl
but the urge for nurture
        is being overwhelmed
  by a nascent drive to devour.

How Death Came into the World

It could be that rabbit was man's enemy
with a wily ruse to introduce death

in the days when the elders of the clan
at the end of their span lay down and slept.

They were placed aside overnight

for spirit to pass over, revitalise.
In the morning they'd wake restored.

But rabbit came by with alternative plan,
boasting of blessing, of bunny abundance,

how burrows and burials are best.

A simple deceit but because man listened,
didn't stick to instructions,

god vented his rage,
                      Death came

Approaching her Birthday

She's scant knowing –

a planned home birth, youngest
of four, a week premature,
hints of heavy weather, relief
she didn't arrive yellow.

Her mother, never one for story-weaving,
no longer alive to supply memories,

she dreams auguries –

a moon-bereft night, piercing shriek
with ghost-winged glide, fox-prints
circumscribe the house, a roof-perched
murmuration flies

as *Snedronningen* veils her mother's eyes,
sets snowdrops in her sight.

Eyrie

No snow, surprisingly, that first winter
her family moved to Scotland
but a spite-spiked wind worrit at fingers
till they bloomed chilblains and toes ballooned
to outgrow boots. She didn't care.
The house was remote as a laird's
with dark oak panels, a spiralling stairway
and picture-flame fires laid by the grey daily,
Mrs McMarneray.
                But what was strange:
her hair turned fair and her bones never grew,
she stayed four foot two for six successive winters
until they flew south one swift summer
borne by wings raised from a sea eagle feather.

How Death Came into the World

It could be in a world facing overpopulation
a choice was given,

either stop copulating or allow Death in.

The gathered men quickly decided
the world would be poorer

without their wisdom,
better no more children.

The women meanwhile, child-caring as usual,
reached a different conclusion,

young ones remind us
mistakes need not bind us,

they cause us to yearn to protect our world.

We will open the door
                      to Death

Mantle

She dreams of knitting a lacy shawl
    in fine 2-ply

the kind that women grow
      through many months

for a baby's christening
    or girl's bottom drawer,

a traditional pattern passed on.

She flicks needles and wool,
      realises her mother's investment,

wonders whether
      her daughters will

survive unshawled.

Not your Daughter

Skull-plastered bag slung on her back
she threads the coast to Cullen Bay:
hair streaked red/jade, nails lacquered black,
skull plastered, bag slung on her back.
Salt-laden pelt as bivouac,
her scythed sea blooms she twists to sprays.
A skull-stashed bag slung from her back
she threads deadheads at Cullen Bay.

Talis-woman

Once artist to tough men with a need
to remember names of mothers or lovers,
mark good luck, betrayal or mythic victory,

he loved to recall how blue dye blubbers
claimed grit under an eyelid,
or memories of a granny's kiss.

Dank nights when jugged he'd blab
of the lass who snuck into his parlour,
five foot three with the air of a pixie.

You'd have heard a needle drop.

He knew he should ask her age, for permission.
But she had the cash and when she told
what she wanted and the position,

willing to reveal in front of the men,
he shooed them all out
except Shy-eye Jim to chaperone him.

Not once did she wince, bottom lip gripped
by elfin teeth till the job was done.
No malice or cockiness, he'd reminisce,

not even rebellion. She strode out the door
wearing the runes of Loki and Thor.
And destruction erupted within him.

Not your Daughter

She stalks the streets of San Tropez,
fists primed for fight, keepsakes to hawk.
The well-heeled, designated prey,
she stalls on streets of San Tropez
to plead her need, make men purvey
her trinkets, wheedling as they walk.
She stalks the streets of San Tropez,
feet primed for flight, fast as a hawk.

Why Drink Lemonade when the Lemons are so Juicy

She tumbles out of bed to a limp and cappuccino,
a smattering of appointments,
her black Labrador waiting to be walked.

She dresses like a fairy but claims herself bewitched,
how else can she explain
the sandpapering in her closet and the jackdaws cawing on the roof.

She says that round abouts there is nobody who knows her,
it's not that kind of locale.
Her neighbours say it's her who blocks the drains.

If asked about her childhood it's a pan boiling over,
a bag of sherbet lemons,
a cactus with outrageous orange blooms.

She says that her escape is a ladder to a loft room
where she can't see the humdrum, can focus on the starshine
and the satellites junking outer space.

Even there she is followed by a straight-haired child of seven
who, lost in a forest, twisted her ankle,
found solace in pelting squirrel dreys.

How Death Came into the World

It could be a woman
designed by the gods

to pay back a man
for stealing fire

was given a jar
stuffed with gifts.

One day, kind of curious,
she unstoppered the lid

and out slipped
       toil and pain,

    hatred and unhappiness
           disease

                  and Death

The Gap Year Trek of Tracey Short

'each passing through, somehow aligned'

She fell for his manner
    in hitching a lift,
the wear-change-wash of his two t-shirts,
  twig-like fingers that could unpick
      any knot or padlock,
squeeze splinters out,
    make strings sing on his grandfather's zither.

He became the lean-on shoulder
    on the all-night bus
 and his full pack of homeland myths
   exiled her memories
in the lingering hours of waiting and riding,
   waiting, riding.

First brother, then lover.

But there were days when his tongue tied,
   his fingers pocket-fasted, eyes hid
     with shades.
She learnt to quell the urge to gabble
   or ask – What is the matter,
 to sit unlocked from their embrace,
  absorb the landscape's messages
      instead of tales,

knew his silences were mirrors
  into which she would not gaze.

No Silver Lining

Kept by her grandmother's faith
she planted seeds at new moon,
sang to the hive in nectar season,

skedaddled away from crowded kitchens,
stayed vigilant for hidden ditches,
saw cows and clouds as wash-day guides.

Yet in that summer of cloudless days
when brooks, then rivers forgot to babble
and carrion birds began to gather,

she awoke one night to a blaze-fury crackle.
She fled following the cackling corvids
but was betrayed by the lore-denied truth,

crows are keepers of circuitous routes.

How Death Came into the World

It could be coyote was none too pleased
that animals died
but humans took turns to reside on earth.

He made his stand at the hut door
in which spirits were recalled
to be embodied.

His snarls and taunts
left spirits shaking,
they emigrated to bodiless haunts.

Coyote lived to regret his action,
when his human son, bitten by a snake,
found no escape

                    from Death

Flight Feathers and Bone

You'd never guess from their couture
they'd flown from a war-torn household,

knew how to pick from reduced-to-clear,
fruit stall's refuse, meat sheened green,

could value any item salvaged
from skip, car boot sale or flea market,

spent youths seeking protection
from the patron saint of stolen coins,

living as pigeons under the bridge
out of the reach of marauding swans.

Ballend Pool

They say this was the drowning place
where churlish men dropped sacked kittens
and guard dogs softened in their heads.

A mile beyond the village bounds
but a wild place
where long-gone glaciers discarded rocks

so the river cascaded in fits and starts
into the pool, so deep they claimed
a monster could writhe in its abyss

and never be seen. Of course,
there were tales of sightings, devourings.
And truer talk –

how mope-headed Jane left her clothes
in a tidy pile at the water's edge, then plunged
to meet her narcissist lover,

and how twins, Lily and Faye, the queerest pair,
with arms entwined, leapt
beyond their father's clutches,

and where, in times of hate, the ducking stool
had loosed its grip on feared wise-women,
hags and witches all.

An ill-will place, they'd say,
and would never come to draw its water
even in the driest years

when village wells were exhausted,
preferring to trek five miles west
than taste its taint.

But that summer,
back from apprenticeship in the town,
with heat fierce as the firing kilns

he stopped listening to gossip, submerged his body
in that cool pool where the river paused,
released its load,

before turbulent tumble to the sea.
Its clarity untangled seared nerves,
quenched a seven-year blaze,

and he learnt the way to return
was not with scorn or sword,
recounting sins as silt on a pool floor

but to let the whispering words of the unheard
enter every pore
and for the dead to be skin to his shadow form.

Lifted

A restlessness possessed, roused her
from her usual pose of comfy chair, a book, a glass of cola
to pace the room, distracted by dis-ease.

Perhaps it was the story's plot or lack thereof,
the summer breeze trapped in her nets
or an animal need to lope.

Whatever had disturbed her, pacing
wasn't enough, the room more dangerous
than her wandering fears as the night drew close.

She left, with cardigan, no coat, without
a backward glance at her neighbours' curtains,
to walk the half mile to the beach,
beset by splaying shadows,
                        lamp trickery.

She found the sea withdrawn, the sun set,
but the sky ablaze,
        vermilion, crimson, tangerine flames,
damask rose clouds darkling mauve,
screaming gulls drawn as silhouetted souls
lost, loved, calling
                calling
                      calling

Sundered, shaped by the moon
        she fetched through the night,
fathomed the wind,

arrived at the dawn
with keening cry, seeing eye, hollow bones.

Classification: *Ursus consolativus*

She's fussing through archives, splitting hairs
over information and record, evidence or representation
whose content, context, structure are authentic.

A den of stashed racks, box upon acid-free box,
all uncatalogued. She must read each document
to locate the one quotation needed for the thesis.

No escape. No *Open Sesame*.
Then his text:
The lovely bones of a living bear.

From mussy hibernation, fur's reek.
She fingers seed, tangle, tick. Finds skin.
Clambers through tissue and vessel to wrap arms

around defined muscle, toes wriggle down femurs.
She nestles against vertebrae, settles in a rib cocoon,
offers honey, pillows his heart.

How Death Came into the World

It could be that presented
with the choice of two bundles

women grabbed the larger
accumulating clutter

of cloth and beads, knives and mirrors,
failing to reflect

that the other contained
escape

        from Death

Running

No-one knew who set them,
       how smooth beds
    became stacked with boulders
          briskening brooks' babbles to brawl.

Some said they were cairns –
      sacred places
sited by a pilgrim on a mission for peace –
     sprinkled salt in penitence.

Others claimed they were devilment,
     impish work,
        clagging
      the course of natural lives.

She wanted to believe in the science of erosion
        but that summer
            they tracked
     from mouth to source

every spot where the current crescendoed
            he slipped her grasp,
      mickle eyed,
    and willing her

              to set him free.

July 23rd

He stirs in the bed, rises. She checks the time,
    sprawls, drifts towards

a Hellish chapter, stones in hands,
    ragefuelled Iagos

chasing imaginings between their sheets.
    Others flee

but she crouches, shelters a child, hopes
    she's unworthy

of their aggression or that the police escort
    is more than warning.

Wrong. A stone hits its mark. She stands
    to protest innocence,

finds an Angel hovering behind,
    arm raised.

Scene change:
    a school gym,

she concocts reasons why swinging
    on power lines

is a selfish decision, and a long-ago friend,
    sticker book in hand,

explains why Disney hasn't a clue about
    structuring fairy tales.

She wakes late, having failed to register
    his exiting revs.

Prey Bird as Neighbour

her presence signalled by shackle-bell tinkle.

Kept for his pleasure
to hood and drive to an open space

to admire sharp eye, keen claw in soar,
spy, pounce. And though the heights

of the food chain are hers to claim
she never resists his lure.

Rule

All cloud-dye day the wasp queen spits her nest
at the base of his linden tree – paper-thin symmetry.

He baits breath, smashes eggshells
on birch trays, patterns mosaics.

Evening sees moth sacrifice by candlelight.
She draws curtains, shuffles the tarot pack.

Faithless he waits, knowing his designs
die or survive with her soothsaying.

How Death Came into the World

It could be that god
     concocted a potion
to make humans immortal.

Snake refused to take.
    The job given to toad
        he hippety-hopped

 hippety-hopped

      hippety-hopped
down the road.

Elixir spilt till none was left
to keep humans

              from Death

Coppicing

She dreams of a home with a secret space:

a vacant priest-hole reached by a spiral stairway behind a door that's revealed when she removes the thirteenth tome from the left on the middle shelf of the oak bookcase,

or an eccentric's cell, locked and coded, stocked with Bunsen burners, test tubes and pipettes, walls lined by bottles with unreadable labels, containing curious liquids with obnoxious smells,

or a subterranean passage to a revolving world, though she's not too fussed about talking animals, fauns or leprechauns.

A house whose walls seem to slide and slip and if she took the time she'd find the dimensions of the rooms didn't match their expected volume.

But her houses have been simple and neat in keeping with their streets. Even her current abode, built in the 1980s, matched its exterior to its aging neighbours, pragmatically fitting in.

Instead she carves chambers in her mind, concealed from the parent, unflappable, sometimes wise; the friend, reliable and kind; the soul-mate, attuned, sacrificial; the work colleague, organised and on schedule; even from the not-yet-famous poet filled with metaphor and ambition.

Crafted, contained, but by turning keys she fosters alternative realities.

> Fallen maiden, stumped
> yet rooted, bathes in new light,
> finds stems multiply.

Constrictive Pericarditis

'Hope deferred makes the heart sick,
but a longing fulfilled is a tree of life.'
Proverbs 13:12

Hard to identify remains, hard to explain
the burnt-out machine, the registration traced to him.

No reason found: an open road, no ice nor rain
nor hairpin bend, no other vehicle on the scene.

'Why him, not her?' the neighbours murmured,
'he full of life, she bound to home.'

They helped her through the necessary motions
to choose the hymns, her clothes, the wreath.

She tossed the first clod in the grave.
Some say she whispered, 'Sweet release.'

At the wake, she wept and raved
about a girl riding bumper cars,

jean-clad lads tossing coins,
sparks, revolutions – a foreign world.

They mollycoddled but weeks passed,
she refused to rally to their good intentions,

shoulders shrugged and fence-talk shifted
to making beds, lying in them.

So no-one noticed that Whitsuntide
a back-packed lass, thorned stick in hand,

uprooting from the town.

To See Through a Glass Darkly

She dreams her body has turned twisting stem,
    sprouting leaves like spindly entrails,
a pillaging foray of foraging elves –
    a tramp tramp trampling three-toed brigade;

a Granny Smith apple snatched from her grasp,
    peeled in one piece, crunched by pixie teeth;

a dappled glade where she lies trapped
    by the barbs of a thousand crow-feather darts
flung by fairies with her friends' features.

She's warned the root is jealousy,
    to mend her ways before it eats her,
in life, it's plain, some are inferior.

But she never reveals the mountain peak,
    precipitous slopes, dancing springs,
a wooden shack not overlooked,

the marionettes,
                      who jerks the strings

Monday's Child is Fair of Face

'Skoll the wolf who shall scare the Moon
Till he flee to the Wood-of-Woe'
WH Auden and PB Taylor

Yoked to Mona she learnt his ways:
                          when to glitter, when to hide,
when to rise anew or embrace decline,
                how to influence the fluxing tides.

She learnt to bask in another's glory,
                swim from ugly duckling into swan,
illumine nursery rhymes, old folk tales,
                  transform her face to tell each story.

She bided time but unattended
                        studied scents, stockpiled furs,
conserved a hoard of Saxon knives,
                  discovered herself more than wife.

Then began the hunt

Reclassification

Not enough to alter appellation,
you must transmute the traits.
So take a rabbit, pluck the scut,

put on a rack. Resect the hop, the urge
to dig a hole, to twitch, to reproduce.
Lengthen the jaw. Insert incisors,

a taste for blood and lust for flesh.
Add padding feet, instinctual howl,
moonshine prowls, a brandished tail.

A final test in headlight glare:
if eyes are steady and do not glaze,
if she snarls then lopes away,

wolf shall be her name.

How Death Came into the World

It could be that chameleon
sent with a message of living forever

couldn't see any hurry
so ambled
        and paused

   ambled
           paused

distracted by his coat of many colours

and a patch of forbidden berries –
ir–re–sist–able.

God, fatalistic,
changed his tune,

commissioned lizard
who scampered   and   skittered

reached man first,
pronounced his sentence
                    of Death

Triptych

Right

By her soft-tongued *Aye* we perceived
    that she was foreign to us.
But she beguiled with tales of times

when women whispered seed to spring,
    trees to fruit, cows to calve,

and country folk paid well
    to feel their charms.

Her songs grew pictures
    of fairs and fetes, of pedlars
        with bright cocks to sell,

whose ribbons lit lacklustre eyes,
    of pennies swopped
        for potions' lies,

and fortune-tellers whose crossed palms
    could chivvy a maid
        towards a man,

persuade a scold to hold her tongue.

We laughed at jesters slipping shit
    beneath the robes of prig and priest,

        at tumblers tossed from pillar
to post who viewed our town
        as upside-down.

But when she spoke
    of fermenting brews
        that could divide a bairn in two
    and leave one stone-cold

    in the womb, the other
        to struggle through its birth,
                arrive a half-wit,

    we paid our dues,

    pronounced sweet blessings
        on her path, pointed
                to the next town.

Acute

Shored by strains of kith and kin
   they cannot ken

each time they still a woman's tongue
   they kill a bairn, make her grow dull

and when they halt an other's song
   they petrify their souls.

Obtuse

Pound, skip, throb,
    tumbling mess,

    hopscotch men,
stone dislodge,

loosen moss
    so jenny wren

has lining for
    her nest.

        Amen.

The Plunderer

He snuck into port, old men shuttered their thoughts
of wanderlust, adventure and gain.
They knew he was the one, by his mischief and fun
who'd cause merriment, mayhem and pain.

How did she come to lie with him
when she knew her love would grieve?
How did she come to lie with him
when she knew he could make her heart bleed?

Though his smile was so charming, his manner disarming,
old men knew he wouldn't be restrained.
He'd break all the rules, to stoke and to fuel
wild passion that coursed through his veins.

How did she come to lie with him
though she knew he lived for his greed?
How did she come to lie with him,
lost to lust, feeling sated and freed?

With a song and a swagger, his dancing dagger
sliced common sense from her brain.
He made captive her heart by that terrible art
of blurring boundaries between crazy and sane.

How did she come to lie with him
entranced by the stories he'd weave?
How did she come to lie with him
forsaking all that she'd believed?

To no-one's surprise as the moon hid her eyes,
they left. Her love postured, complained,
made impotent gestures about how he'd fetch her
till old men's lips curled in disdain.

How did she come to rely on him,
when she knew he cheated and thieved?
All she knew was she'd willingly die for him
for he thrust to the core of her need.

Deathblow

'Dead men tell no tales'

He'd just settled down,
laid next to his wife,
for a good long rest,
glad to be free
of the struggle and strife.

He'd endured the wake,
its wailing shenanigans,
heard how he was loved,
how missed he'll not be.

He guessed one day,
though God knows when,
he'd be called up
by a trumpet blast
or the earth shaking.

But he wasn't expecting
this recent revival,
dragged from the ground
in the dead of night
to be gaped at by strangers,
slit skin flapped apart,
all his innards outer.

And as for his Annie
they've felt more of her
than he ever managed.

The Elizabethan Coast

In the year of our Lord 1588
Brabanter Stevenson fetched up,
promising rich pickings
to tempt men to work the copperas.
In Tankerton fish were the living
but with no stomach for swell and squall,
Joe joined the gang, dug the pits,
collected the fossil twigs,
kept them bucked with seawater –
for four years!
                That Brabanter paid well
and when he began to sell to wool
and leather men, engravers and quacks,
he was true to his word – Joe's money grew.

But it's devil's brew! Tom slid a stone
in his pocket. By the time he was home
his gabardine was burned and holed.
And Harry, the fool, fell in the trough.
They fished him fast – but that night
he breathed his last.
                Aye, strange business!
The Dutchman, though, proved shrewd,
knew the worth of biding time,
showed living as more than hand-to-mouth.

How Death Came into the World

It could be there was a rope
  for when people felt old

to ascend to heaven,
  gain rejuvenation

before zipping back to earth
  to continue their work.

Sneaky hyena, wanting a peak
  at heavenly wonders,

shinned up, found himself captured.
    Hyena masterminded

his escape...

sliced through the rope
  once he'd abseiled its length.

So, humans no longer are revitalised
but remain on earth

              until Death

A Stitch in Time

'It'll soon be stitched up.' Sitting cross-legged on the path, blocking her jog, his needle darted across the hole in last week, specifically Tuesday evening when round at Cassie's the Mojitos flowed and she'd no idea how she got home. But rents and slashes were elsewhere too. 'Some go for elaborate embroidery – satin and feather, cross and chain – like that chap in Bayeux, wanting his slant on the story. Me, I just cobble. Or use blanket stitch to overlock seams. One trick is to buttonhole it – soonest mended that way. You never knew? It's been happening since the beginning of history. Take a look at the canvas and you'll see woven threads. Better to patch than blot, you'll agree. I'm of ancient lineage – The Missing Links – no tailoring too big or small. Desperate times just warrant greater creativity – snip into pieces, re-pattern in patchwork.'

His chatter paused as he unravelled a new thread, tied a knot in one end, eyed up the needle. She skirted round to continue her route but as she glanced back, he shouted, 'Running's OK, but if you get a stitch... Y'hear the headline this week? A seamstress in Pinn saves nine.'

A Thanet Fable

Hengist and Horsa and their able-bodied men
sailed across the water to meet King Vortigern.
They journeyed from Jutland in the year 449,
bringing Rowena, Hengist's daughter, to be Vortigern's bride.

But you shouldn't trust a dragon when it sails into your port,
a dragon's fierce, a dragon's free and won't do as it ought.

The king was having trouble with a brutish bunch of Picts
pillaging and plundering and a pick of treacherous tricks.
To secure Saxon aid, he promised Thanet for their home
but those fiery-bellied warriors had some ideas of their own.

Oh, you shouldn't trust a dragon when it sails into your port,
a dragon's fierce, a dragon's free and won't do as it ought.

Vortigern surmised that if he married Hengist's daughter,
he would wield the power over those dragons of the water,
but as they were victorious in fight after fight,
Vortigern had to ponder if his premise had been right.

No, you shouldn't trust a dragon when it sails into your port,
a dragon's fierce, a dragon's free and won't do as it ought.

On the day Horsa was slaughtered, Vortigern wept with relief,
but Hengist's grief-fuelled anger fired in him a new belief
that he only could be happy if he were king of Kent.
So Vortigern discovered what those whispered rumours meant

Which said, you shouldn't trust a dragon when it sails into your port,
a dragon's fierce, a dragon's free and won't do as it ought.

Hengist quickly vanquished all the people of the land
and Kent became a kingdom under Saxon command.
The moral of the story? Don't trade Thanet for some Picts
or the folk of Thanet might select a different way to live.

For you shouldn't trust a dragon when it sails into your port,
a dragon's fierce, a dragon's free and won't do as it ought.

In 1949 the Danes sailed back to our land.
Hugin the dragon beached on Broadstairs Main Sands
which promptly changed its name to become Viking Bay
and the ship is perched in Pegwell, a memento of those days.

But now we keep the dragon that sailed into our port,
so we'll be fierce, we'll be free and we won't do as we ought.

For when you've caught the dragon that sails into your port,
then you'll be fierce, you'll be free and you won't do as you ought.

Hooden Horsing Around

For a week every year
a retiring seaside town shifts gear
as a shuffling, shantying, jingling set
wave handkerchiefs and play slap sticks.

Men overgreened, in crow-crowned hats
or garlanded with flowers and leaves,
escort rouged ladies with beards and curls,
in bovver boots and nylon slips.

You might spot a pirate come ashore,
morris majors and minors on promenade,
clogged-up lasses or weaving Scots
crooning ballads of lust and loss

in tent, marquee, school, church or pub,
they dine on ale, fish'n'chips and fudge,
play fiddle, flute and slide guitar,
melodeon, spoons or ukulele,

amplified or improvised,
solo hotshots, carousing choirs
with restless festive formation feet,
as though all folk are overcome

with red shoes dancing syndrome.
And through the week you best beware
of blackened stallions stalking streets
to hoodwink for a kiss.

As Luck Would Have It

Once a farmer owned a horse
which he rode and worked in his fields.
One day his horse escaped to the hills.
The neighbours rushed to sympathise,
How awful! How terrible! What rotten bad luck!

> The farmer shrugged and simply said,
> *Bad luck? Good luck? Who can tell?*
> *All we can do is to try to live well.*

For a week the neighbours muttered
about how the farmer wouldn't get his crops sown.
But the horse knew on which side its bread was buttered
(sorry, poor metaphor – where its oats were grown),
so returned to the farm with some pals it had made,
a herd of wild horses galloped in and stayed.
The neighbours rushed to congratulate,
Free horses! Such blessing! Such bounteous good luck!

> The farmer shrugged and simply said,
> *Good luck? Bad luck? Who can tell?*
> *All we can do is to try to live well.*

The farmer had an only son
who was strong, lithe and capable.
The son began to tame those horses,
whispering and riding them into submission.
But a spirited stallion tossed the young man
who landed badly and broke his leg.
The neighbours rushed to sympathise,
How awful! How terrible! What rotten bad luck!

> The farmer shrugged and simply said,
> *Bad luck? Good luck? Who can tell?*
> *All we can do is to try to live well.*

One day the army marched through the land
conscripting young men for their fight.
The son limped along, dragging his leg.
'No use,' thought the captain, 'he'll never keep up.'
So sent him back home to his father.
The neighbours rushed to congratulate,
He'll be well before harvest! Such blessing! Such luck!

    But the farmer shrugged and simply said,
    Good Luck? Bad Luck? Who can tell?
    All we can do is to try to live well.

How Death Came into the World

It could be dog and goat are tasked
with letting Life pass

but preventing Death.

Goat goads dog,
'You'll soon start to doze.'

Dog disagrees,
shows boundless energy
by leaping about, chasing his tail.

The argument escalates till goat,
offended by dog's innuendoes,

                    butts out.

Dog keeps watch, paces up and around,
reckons he deserves a little lie-down.

Soon grunts and snores prove him asleep.

                          Death creeps past

Strand

Years later
      she remembered how he introduced
  outdoor feasts –
                          no rigmarole –
a tin-tray BBQ sparked by cigarette lighter,
  foil-wrapped fish and fruit.

               And while they baked,
a penknife produced avocado halves,
     slices of lemon squeezed for juice.

Slipped from his pocket,
                the teaspoon for feeding.

Fish flaking perfection fit into pittas
  with cherry tomatoes

                before pear
and peach, each mouth-lusting piece
  just right for two bites.

             And all the time
the lulling lap of an ebbing tide
                       reminding

The Weed-Reaper

Sunset fade from rose to grey   sea perfect charcoal sheen
slow-coming with the flow   air-prow boat   barely seakeeping.

Balanced in the stern   bailing   bailing   tillering past
scuppering jags   dragging the tangle.

Salt-savvy   he plies sea-sufficiency   nutrients
for land & beast   supply the drench for pelagic dreams.

In this Frostless Land

beyond the cross-bearing barren field
the old man's beard covers bare forms,
frail silver ladies, needing neighbourly support,
lose their grip, lie broken limbed,
matrons flock, bleat about smirched fleeces,
and in sodden pasture mackintoshed mares are put out.

Jack

he claimed
though none knew who named him

but it fit
        with his life at sea
  how he'd filch plums
            leave no lass lean

soothetongue   darestrong

oh he could ferret any jill
        tumble up or
            down hill

make men feel they'd sealed the deal
                      but his flung seeds
found fertile ground
    sprouted   and grew

    waybeat   footfleet

he'd plucked the hen
      from a Big Man's table

sunder a sloth from his gold

    bragharp   stingsharp

but once he crowed
    he'd crossed the devil
   bartered   his soul
      for tree reprieve

    waybarred   feartfar

       he turned jackdaw
cackcoat   woodfloored

  the day he died

   coaltossed   hardfrost

turnip flamefaces
     flighted his wraith

Winter's Code

'Three black oaks rear through the snow:
Rough, but nimble-fingered.'
Tomas Tranströmer (tr. Robin Robertson)

Grandmother claimed each New Year's Eve the black oaks
became freed stallions galloping the snow-clad moor.

Grandfather claimed the oaks were witches
whose nimble fingers were full of tricks.

Grandmother said these reckless beauties would never be ridden,
tails and manes in flight, they swept out the old year.

Grandfather said when we thought we heard creaking tree limbs,
it was really the cackling of cast spells.

Grandmother insisted where hoof-prints dinted the frozen earth,
these were the places snowdrops sprang forth.

Grandfather replied it was fiery eyes that melted snow,
wand sorcery that caused new growth.

Who to believe? Most gently scoffed,
murmured about age-addled brains.

Until Jimmy McFaine, whisky-speaking, coal in hand
set off to first-foot, declaring his first stop

would be the black oaks, they could wish him luck.
When we said, 'Don't be daft,'

he bragged he wasn't afraid of fireside tales.
Well, neither were we.

But next day his body was found, hung by the hair
from the middle tree, ten feet off the ground.

How it got there, nobody knew.
But that year we learnt in every tale is an acorn of truth.

Laid Bare

On first hearing, you'd be forgiven
for thinking this is some well-oiled yarn
spun through countless generations
sat around winter fires, the only heat
that keeps their souls alive. A tale beginning,
Once long ago, last week I saw...
perhaps featuring Baba Yaga,
tricking youths and testing maidens,
or maybe Snegurochka, melted by love.

This story starts with two elderly sisters,
young in their grief, they're battling
through bitter winds and treacherous snowdrifts,
with tears icicled on their cheeks.
They clutch, not flowers, this arctic wasteland
provides no such blessing, but a brush
to sweep the snowfall
from their brother's fresh-dug grave.

Almost upon that place, they freeze,
startled to see a stranger kneeling, moaning,
keening. Wrapped in bedraggled fur,
he furiously scrapes at the frozen earth.
Alarmed at such violent grief
the sisters hide beneath nearby trees,
realise, too late, this stranger is no man
but an ancient forest one – black bear.

If this were a tale, a homespun one,
perhaps with moral purpose or woven wisdom,
black bear would be there to release
their brother's soul to roam his beloved forest.
Instead, we find this is some wily beast,
who having come upon a giant fridge,
munches a scavenged lunch.

How Death Came into the World

It could be that rabbit was man's enemy
with a wily ruse to introduce death.

He arrived at the door with a peace offering,
some tasty tree roots that he'd uncovered
whilst digging his burrow.

A precious gift, he insisted,
failing to mention their poisonous nature.
So when man roasted and ate

                          Death came

Reflection

'I've wanted so many lives
such otherness'
John Burnside

Not able to master (or mistress) one
    but flitting between   parent   orphan
        goddess   demon   alien

never staying in one place for roots to thrive
  but setting chase
      as a child dashes after bubbles

not saddened by each bursting
    but eager for the next   the next   the next
      their rainbows sparkling in the sun.

What lives could have been lived
    may be will live

with   courage   chance   circumstance
    change of wind's direction
    are blossom doomed for puddles.

But we'll not convince the self that dreams
  of other lives
      that our trajectories

hold   significance   order   mystery
    until we find our obituaries

read our selves
      as others always have.

Acknowledgements

Thanks are due to Simon Barraclough: the poems *How Death Came into the World* emerged from a Poetry School course tutored by him. Thanks and acknowledgements are also due to the editors of the following publications in which some of these poems have appeared: *Canterbury Festival Poet of the Year Anthology, Confluence, Loose Muse Anthology of New Writing by Women, Message in a Bottle, Not Only the Dark: 160 poems on the theme of survival, Pop-Up Poetry Anthology, Snakeskin, The Journal;* and to the judge of the Saveas Poetry Competition, 2013, who deemed 'Classification: *Ursus consolativus*' worthy of first prize.